NORWEGIAN SKETCH BOOK
JOURNEY TO THE TOP OF THE WORLD

A LIMITED EDITION Nº 149 OF 500

Happy Birthday Barbara January 2000
Brian Tanner + Pam xx

Published 1999 by Brian Edwards, The Coach House, Main Street,
Great Longstone, Derbyshire DE45 1TZ, England
Tel: +44 (0) 1629 640752
Fax: +44 (0) 1629 814745
Email: brianedwardsgl@talk21.com

Printed and bound by J.W. Northend Ltd.
Clyde Road, Sheffield, S8 OTZ, England
Tel: +44 (0) 114 250 0331
Fax: +44 (0) 114 250 0676
Web site: www.northend.co.uk
Email: info@northend.co.uk
ISDN: +44 (0) 114 250 7814

A catalogue record of this book is available from
the British Library

ISBN 0 952 5064 5 9

Text, illustrations, photographs and design by
Brian Edwards

FOREWORD

On this the most beautiful voyage on the Polarlys during May of 1999, we had the great pleasure to become acquainted with Brian Edwards. During the whole tour we saw him energetically catching the beauty and poetry of the Norwegian coast with his pen and brush.

This collection of his drawings and paintings, put together in a book, will give us lifelong memories from a unique voyage.

Ingebjørg and Arvid Tjeldnes, Norwegian Tour Leader, Oslo.

This book is dedicated to my brother Geoff Edwards, who spent a lifetime selflessly encouraging others, myself included, and was allowed far too little time to reap the benefits of early retirement. Ironically, he and I were to collaborate on our first book together – he was a fine writer and poet – but we simply were not allowed the privilege. He and Margaret's love for that once Norwegian territory of Sutherland produced much fine poetry. I am proud to start my voyage with these apt words:

So engrossed
in watching the leaf
fall,
like a tear
from the tree,
I almost failed
to notice
that,
when it touched
the brow of the
lake,
it spread a smile
across the face
of the water.

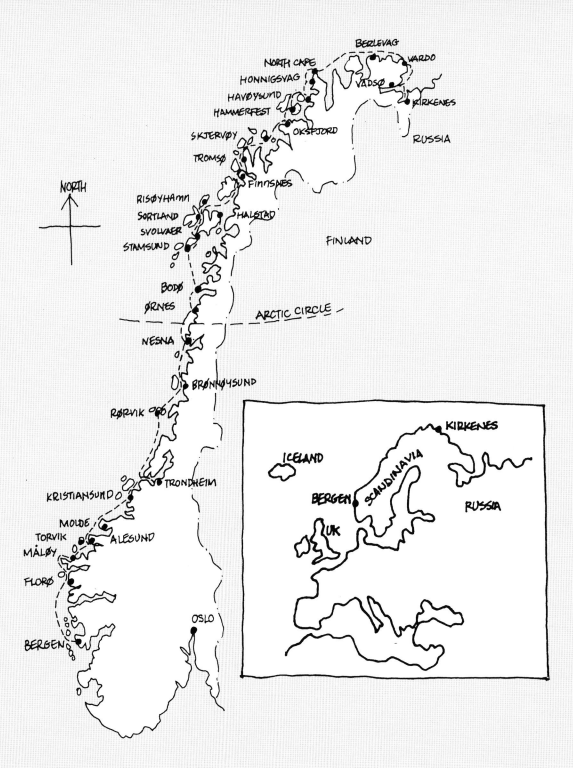

NORTH

BERLEVAG
NORTH CAPE
VARDO
HONNIGSVAG
VADSØ
HAVØYSUND
KIRKENES
HAMMERFEST
OKSFJORD
RUSSIA
SKJERVØY
TROMSØ
FINNSNES
RISØYHAMN
SORTLAND
HALSTAD
SVOLVAER
STAMSUND
FINLAND
BODØ
ØRNES
ARCTIC CIRCLE
NESNA
BRØNNØYSUND
RØRVIK
TRONDHEIM
KRISTIANSUND
MOLDE
TORVIK
ÅLESUND
MÅLØY
FLORØ
OSLO
BERGEN

ICELAND
KIRKENES
BERGEN
SCANDINAVIA
UK
RUSSIA

INTRODUCTION

They all said "don't be daft, you on a cruise, you the hyperactive, you who never learnt to sit still for a minute; you'll be jumping overboard and swimming alongside". Privately I agreed but the decision was made following a major operation for my wife Pam.

Of course, when it turned out to be the most amazing of holidays, it was all my idea; that's the way it is in our relationship.

After a flight to Bergen and the best part of two days in one of the most interesting and challenging cities I have been to, we embarked for a remarkable trip to North Cape, truly the top of the world.

On the first day I awoke with a start at 4.45am as the boat manoeuvred into a small village quayside. The light was phenomenal and I tore into my clothes and stumbled up to the deck. Outside, in the cool dawn light, all was still apart from the unloading and loading of our ship, the Polarlys. I soon fetched my sketchbook to record the scene with pen and aquarelle water colour pencils. And that set the scene for the next eleven days. Every opportunity to record our voyage was taken as we steamed some 2500 miles (4000 kms) alongside snowcapped Norwegian mountains and through dramatic islands with jagged peaks thrusting over 3000 feet (1000mtrs) straight out of the mirrored sea.

You see, I am a professional illustrator and I had decided that this would not be another assignment, it was a holiday. But my mind was racing with the ever changing images; did I get fed up with mountains and islands day after day? Not a bit, for every five minutes the scenery was changing as we purred through the last throws of the Gulf Stream. I was soon joined by a fellow 'hyperactive', a Norwegian Tour Organiser in his seventies, born in the remote Lofoten Islands, steeped in Viking exploits, mythology, anger with the devastation of World War II, and full too with the romanticism of literature and his adventures under sail. He explained his boyish enthusiasm with "I wake up each day and feel that this is another day of opportunity". As I sketched, he described vividly all about the passing scenery. My sketching and painting, and his chatter, were almost non-stop. The patterns of our wake, the glorious sunsets, the busy fishing boats, the isolated communities at water's edge, were all subjects of the poetry of tongue and pen. Most of all I learnt the importance of fishing in the history of Norway, the lives it had taken, the hardships, the triumphs, the romantic image of lonely man pitting his wits against the savage sea, the grieving widow and orphans (epitomised in countless sculptures throughout Norway). For it is in the winter that the cod is abundant and brought home to hang out and dry on communal racks before their export to exotic countries in the Far East, South America and Iberia. "Catholic countries, you see, they keep the fishing viable in these far away lands".

We slipped into small communities and Northern Cities well beyond the Arctic Circle and were surprised with the quality of both traditional and modern architecture of Trondheim and Tromsø, having left far to the south the more accessible and wonderful Art Nouveau town of Ålesund. We enjoyed the majesty of soaring rocks and turquoise water in the Trollfjord and wondered at the skill of the captain who turned this huge ship round on itself only feet away from the brown granite cliffs which were split by torrents jetting down from hidden heights.

The Lofoten Islands, well up into Arctic seas, are a 60 mile length of precipitous peaks and clusters of tiny, sea-pounded islets, with a few communities still partly reliant on the God-like cod but much dependent on tourism. That does not stop the acceptance of modern technology as a matter of pride. "We were pioneers of the telegraph, telephone and electricity. Nowadays we have so much hydro-electricity that our vast reserves of natural gas are sold aboard, we have no need of it."

Still the pen raced and the brush stroked the sketchbooks, paper discarded every ten minutes or so as yet another dramatic mountain or island formation came into view. "The sea is so treacherous around here, with thousands of rocks hidden just below the surface, that the Vikings preferred to carry their great long boats over high mountains rather that risk their lives sailing down the treacherous coast."

It is hard to equate these grizzled macho warriors with the modern Norwegian husband who is obliged to take his share of maternity leave, thus substituting the longboat for a smart pram.

Every one of the sixty or so stops on the voyage prompted a rush out into the crisp, yet, mild air to capture the environment of these far flung communities. One day it happened, I suppose I half expected it. Arvid, my new found Norwegian friend asked if I had thought of putting the sketches and water colours into a book, a visual diary of our voyage. The project grew in his animated mind and the book became reality as he scurried round the passengers selling the idea and encouraging orders. His wife and my wife joined in, our tour manager encouraged the plan and there it was born.

Perhaps I should emphasise that these illustrations are from my sketchbooks and were never intended as "finished" drawings and wherever I was unable to sketch something of interest I have added colour photographs from the large number taken by myself.

Well here is the result of my labours and I hope you will enjoy it. For those who have been on this amazing voyage perhaps it will bring back happy memories. If you have not been then perhaps I will have persuaded you to sail on the Hurtigruten!

Brian Edwards

Our good ship 'Polarlys' towers above the quaysides. The curved top set of windows are those of the Panorama Lounge, where I would sit well into the night, astounded at the beautiful skies, whenever the ship was approaching port or when we had warning of something spectacular ahead. The fine May weather meant that most days I could sketch from the open stern deck where it was sheltered and there the view was over the fascinating patterns of the ship's wake.

7

Bergen is a delightful town full of interesting old wooden buildings painted in a wide range of colours. Bryggen is the name of the old wharf area, a major trading centre from as early as the 13th century. These timeworn warehouses and factories now house a variety of artists and craftsmen.

BRYGGEN IN BERGEN

BRIAN EDWARDS 1999

GRIEG'S HOUSE BERGEN BRIAN EDWARDS 1999

The home of Edward Grieg, the Norwegian composer, was built in 1885 at Troldhaugen near Bergen. The tranquil setting overlooking an inlet must surely have been to Grieg, as it was to me, an inspiration. The composer's cottage below the house is a few metres above the waters of the fjord; what a place to be creative.

Having set sail from Bergen in the late evening I awoke at 4.45am and looked out on the tiny village of Florø. The view prompted the first of many sketches throughout the voyage. This page from one of my sketchbooks shows that I noted still waters and snow-capped mountains as the ship loaded and unloaded pallets full of supplies.

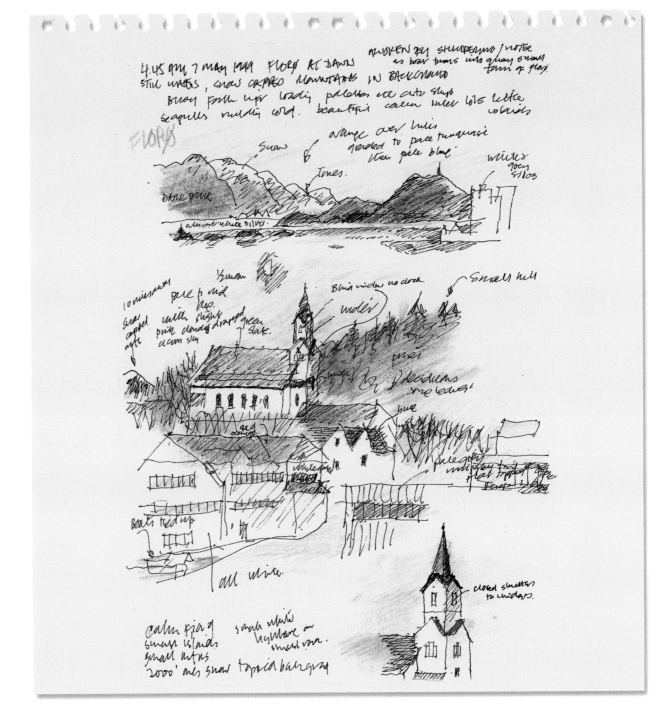

9.30AM 7 MAY ALONG THE COAST TO TORVIK CONSTANT HEADLANDS & INLETS STRONG SUN TONAL SHADING BLINDINGLY BRIGHT REFLECTION SUN ONTO SEA. BRIAN EDWARDS.

1256

There was a strange
light as we worked
along the coast
towards Torvik.
I noted that the strong
sun threw blinding
reflections onto the
surface of the water.

Distant views of snow-clad mountains and closer views of tiny communities at the water's edge. Just here it is so difficult to know exactly what is mainland and what is island. We thread our way through Nordfjord to Måløy,

HEADLAND NEAR MALØY 8.30 7 APRIL 1999 (MALØY RASET)

BRIAN EDWARDS

1266

PULLING OUT INTO THE OCEAN FROM NORDFJORD   BRIAN EDWARDS

1268

ON THE WAY TO ALESUND
11.30 AM 7/6/99 BRIAN EDWARDS 12.69

On the way to Ålesund where we were due to stay for three hours – couldn't wait to get off and explore. Throughout Western Norway, sculptures on a fishing theme are justifiably in evidence and they depict grieving orphans, widows and fish packers. Ålesund is no exception.

FISHERMAN SCULPTURE AT ALESUND 1999
BRIAN EDWARDS.

Ålesund is rich in well-preserved Art Nouveau architecture, thanks to a major fire which spread through the town in 1904. We climbed to the top of Aksla Mountain where we had a picnic lunch and also ate up the panoramic view which included the Polarlys. Then we explored the inner harbour area we found quite delightful. Not much time to sketch.

APPROACHING MOLDE. 3.30PM 7/5/99.   BRIAN EDWARDS

APPROACHING MOLDE 5.15 PM 7/5/99   BRIAN EDWARDS

We were really in Viking territory as we left Ålesund. To the west is the island of Giske, home of the great chieftains, and I had a strong urge to jump ship and investigate, (but not to rape and pillage). Soon we crossed the Romsdalfjord and approached Molde.

Molde is another place where we could get off the ship and in this case take a well worth coach tour, aiming to link up with the ship some hours later. The waterfront is dominated with a vast new football stadium which was donated I believe by a rich expatriate. We had a magnificent view over the fjord towards a chain of mountains with over two hundred and twenty peaks; reminded me a little of the view over Lake Geneva. I scribbled away as the guide poured out facts... reconstructed old town, outdated wooden ski jumps, horticultural delights of the judge's garden, and another fishy sculpture.

Molde 5.35 pm 7/5/99.

Our coach took us through fascinating and surprisingly fertile landscape bordering the sea and stopped briefly at Bud with its preserved German WWII bunkers. As I looked out to sea I could see our ship in the distance and realised why this was such a strategic location. Over the next few hours we were very much aware that, as we worked our way up the coast, we were being shadowed by the Polarlys some half mile offshore. Cloud capped, steep sided mountains loomed ahead and we were told that the waters offshore were so treacherously dotted with partly submerged rocks that the Vikings preferred to carry their longboats over tough peaks rather than face the sea route. There was a stop for traditional fish dinner in the hamlet of Storholmen, with food, service and views all delicious. Next we headed over the Atlantic Ocean Road with it's eight spectacular bridges connecting the large island group of Averøya with the mainland. What a drive that must be in harsh weather.

After rejoining the ship late evening in Kristiansund, we reached Trondheim in the early morning for a six hour stay. Pam and I set off at great pace, exploring the old suburbs, climbing up to the 17th century fortress and guessing that this would provide us with a clear view of the city. Then via the riverbank to the Nidaros Cathedral part dated from the 12th century. It was Sunday – sad that museums and galleries only opened later in the day.

On the return trip we looked around the old wooden wharf buildings and the quite elegant and compact city centre, which we much admired.

In my sketchbook I noted, as we left Trondheim, that we passed Monks Island, once the home of he Benedictines and later a prison.

TRONDHEIM BYARKERKKINKS

I am quite sure that the fortress was keeping a close eye on us as we climbed towards it! We found the centre of Trondheim well endowed with interesting old buildings and modern design too. Once away from Trondheim, the mountains gave way to skerries and small islands, much softer, with green hills and groups of red roofed farms.

1 PM 8/5/99 ½HR FROM TRONDHEIM. THE LANDSCAPE SOFTENS, LOWER HILLS FARMS + HOUSES.

1248

The early morning. It's getting serious now. This is the southernmost point where the midnight sun shines for 24 hours on midsummer night's eve.

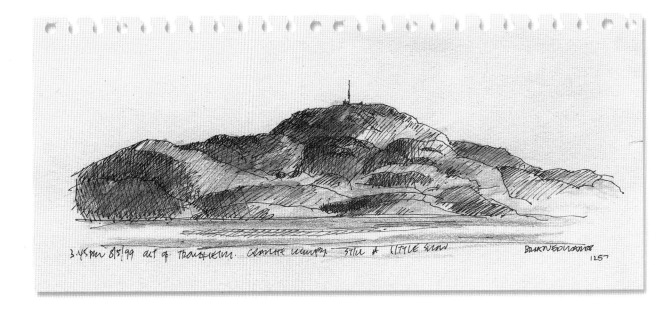

3.45pm 8/5/99 out of Trondheim. Granite mountains still a little snow. BRIAN EDWARDS 1257

NEAR ØRNES. BRIAN EDWARDS 1999. 1250

Hestmann Island, the Horseman mentioned in the saga on page 64.

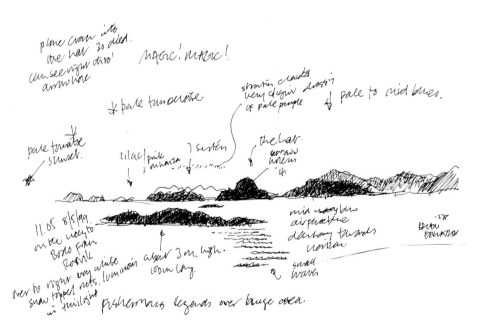

A typical page of scribbled reminders.

Throughout the voyage there were clusters of fisherman's huts with what looked like, but couldn't be, rather rickety landing stages covered with the paraphernalia of the trade. The little boats were usually clustered so closely together that it was hard to distinguish one from the other.

TYPICAL FISHERMANS HOUSES   BRIAN EDWARDS 1991

1391

BRIAN EDWARDS
JUMBLE OF FISHING BOATS 1999

ØRNES 9.45 KM 9/6/1996   BRIAN EDWARDS   1249.

Near Ørnes the
surroundings became
quite precipitous with
snow on the
mountain tops.

Still there were
mountains closing in.

AM. 10.20 9.5.95 ROUNDING THE END OF THE FJORD AT ØRNES   HOT SUN PLACID FJORD ALL BROWNS BLUES PURPLES   1259
BRIAN EDWARDS.

AM. 11.30 DITTO.
BRIAN EDWARDS.

1260

Hot sun – the
mountains were
browns, blues and
purples.

Strangely shaped mountains on the way to Bodø where we had a couple of hours ashore. Busy harbour and airport, administrative and college centre for the Nordland area.

11.20 AM ON THE WAY TO BODO ALMOST CLOUDLESS PALE BLUE SKY CALM SEA.
BRIAN EDWARDS.

many more peaks ←

LOFOTEN ISLANDS 6pm 9/5/99. RISING 2000 FT out of sea forms an Atlantic wall and shelter until winds blow from south west. About 5 hours sail from mainland and all snowcapped clear blue skies except for white grey clouds hovering above. This is just a small section of the panorama. Dark airforce blue sea few white horses.

BRIAN EDWARDS   1255

We crossed open sea for three hours and the Lofotveggan loomed as a chain of islands, forming a wall of peaks some 100kms (over 60 miles) in length – my sketchbook wasn't wide enough. We now entered the major cod grounds. Mesmerised by the magnetic pull of the Lofotens – more on the return journey.

During the night we threaded our way through narrow channels, I just didn't want to miss anything, little sleep. Between the islands and late morning we crossed the Vagsfjorden and arrived in Finnsnes having passed Harstad with the 'Adolf Gun' perched on the hill above the church – a reminder yet again of WWII.

HEADING NORTH FROM FINNESNES 12.40 10/5/99   HOT NO WIND PATCHY SKY VERY CALM, LOTS OF FLATTS DOTTED
AROUND GENTLY SLOPING SHORE.   BRIANEDWARDS

1262

10/6/99 1pm
LEAVING FINNESNES. BEHIND   BRIANEDWARDS
                                                                    1263

We were well into the trip and had three hours ashore in Tromsø, a busy trading centre with many delightful attractions. Quite a lot of snow around – compact town centre with several interesting buildings – boats and ships to-ing and fro-ing, we viewed the waterside activity from a café in the new user-friendly indoor shopping centre (unlike the many dreadful ones in England). We were much impressed with Tromsø.

At first we wondered what on earth had happened – had a pile of giant books collapsed? On closer examination we realised it was the new Polar Museum with a shop full of beautifully crafted products.

POLAR MUSEUM TROMSØ BRIANEDWARDS 1999.

(32)

TROMSØ ATTRACTIVE POSITION AND TOWN –
CATHEDRAL + POLAR MUSEUM WHICH IS LIKE
A ROW OF BOOKS FALLING OVER.

PLEASANT HOUSES FROM EARLY 20TH CENTURY
USUALLY WHITE WOODEN + WITH BALCONIES.
OLD CHURCH + SQUARE INTERESTING AND
HARBOUR EXTENSIVE ALONG THE FRONT.
IMPRESSIVE BRIDGE ACROSS FIORD.

CATHEDRAL OF THE ARCTIC - TROMSDALEN CHURCH TROMSØ   BRIAN EDWARDS 1999   1326.

CATHEDRAL AT TROMSØ '630 10/5/99,

A distant view of 'The Arctic Cathedral' – the Tromsdalen church – led to a walk across the 1000 metres long bridge over the Tromsøysundet which gave us the opportunity to view the magnificent stained glass window – Europe's largest glass mosaic. The cracks in the concrete walls made us slightly nervous. Nearby was a group of splendid old wooden houses.

FROM HAMMERFEST HARBOUR 11/5/99

We sailed into
Hammerfest through
a narrow channel
accompanied by
calm seas and clear
blue skies.

HAMMERFEST MAY 1999   BRIAN EDWARDS

HAMMERFEST

BRIAN EDWARDS 1999.

The scribbling in my sketchbook notes: Hammerfest 6.30am 11th May 1999 – in a bay surrounded by low hills. Plenty of snow – lots of packaged pallets, loaded with mixed goods from cornflakes to electrical goods, taken off whilst crates of soft drinks etc. loaded on. Quite a lot of activity. Hammerfest is remarkable only that it exists so far north, more utilitarian than pretty. Wide range of up-to-date goods in shops. Snowmobiles parked in gardens – someone had a large World War II gun in theirs. Quite sunny and relatively mild. Hammerfest is close to the Russian border and was once famous for the fur trade – said to be, until recently, most northern town in the world.

How on earth do you sketch from a bus twisting round bends on the way to North Cape? With difficulty I can assure you. We had left the ship at Honningsvag where a huddle of wooden houses clinging to the mountainside were protected by avalanche fences. Across the bay an oil terminal did not intrude.

My notebook tells me that we were 16 hours by boat from Tromsø but only an hour by plane. Also that there are 500 different types of rock here – and industrial diamonds.

NORTH CAPE NORWAY MAY 1999 BRIAN EDWARDS.

North Cape. "This is where the world ends and this is where my curiosity ends, and I can return home satisfied" so wrote Italian Pietro Negri in 1664. It is a desolate place, rather an anticlimax. Crossing over a snow-covered plateau to reach the headland, we passed herds of reindeer – I guess it looked rather like the Peak District (although we have red and roe deer here) Too cold to do much sketching but revived by a warm coffee at the intriguing museum.

Sailing EAST! We passed the Finnkjerka or Church Rock, nice but not spectacular yet a diversion in this black and white, chilly world.'Surprise, surprise' I note, at Kinnarodden, we were even further north than North Cape. Soon we were sailing south to Vadsø and then Kirkenes where we were to turn around.

11/5/99 8pm CHURCH ROCK

1279

BEYOND NORTH CAPE.

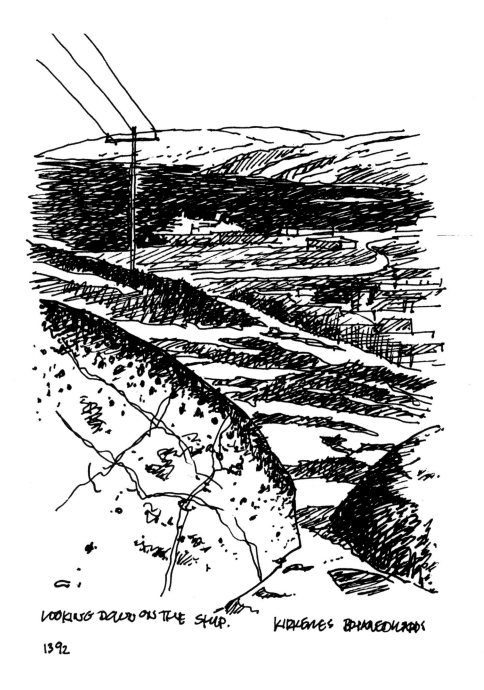

LOOKING DOWN ON THE SHIP.   KIRKENES BACKGROUNDS

1392

At Kirkenes we were only a few miles from Russia and close to Finland too. Like so many Norwegian towns and villages, Kirkenes was razed to the ground in 1944. Here we had time to walk up a hill overlooking the town but to get to the best vantage point had to trudge knee-deep in snow from one outcrop to another. Amazingly, for its fairly hostile position, Kirkenes is quite attractive in parts and surrounded by stretches of water. We could see that Kvaerners have a factory here; they bought up part of Sheffield's steel industry too. Dumbfounded as to why anyone would want to live up there.

Near Kirkenes, there were ice floes in the water, a few whales too and a couple of rusty Russian freighters. Strangely the water was quite calm but almost devoid of reflections.

CURIOUS STRUCTURE MAY 1999
NORWAY   BRIAN EDWARDS

VARDØ 5pm 12/5/99 CALM SEA GETTING CLOUDY.

VARDØ 2.

Moving fast into
Vardø – I liked the
contrast between the
modern shapes and
the more traditional
silhouettes behind.

Vardø is a surprisingly interesting town. Completely gutted during the war but has at least two interesting churches and an old octagonal fort from 1737. Best viewpoint meant standing in snow.

BRIAN EDWARDS 1999

CHURCH AT VARDO NORWAY WITH GUNS

SUNSET/SUNRISE 12/5/99.
VARDØ.

Calm peaceful sea
out of Vardø – here
the midnight sun
goes down and
straight back up
again – or is it merely
a reflective trompe
d'oeil? One fishing
boat was drenched in
sea birds.

The midnight sun went up, or was it down, at Berlevåg with it's French built breakwater. A small island had some sort of structure – looked like a submarine, and the sun was parted by a small streak of cloud. How lucky we continued to be with the weather, perfect.

Ham coming out of Havøysund fairly calm – village was better than the last one – nice church, more compact, smaller medium calm plenty of sun despite clouds. nice fishing huts. snow on streets. average house about 70k.

At noon we sailed into Hammerfest again through a narrow channel, clear blue sky and moderately calm sea. The Norwegians sure know how to organise holidays.

The food on board was heavenly, fresh salmon, smoked salmon, all sorts of mouth-watering delicacies by the ton.

3PM 13/5/99 ON THE WAY TO ØKSFJORD FROM HAMMERFEST SPARKLING MEDIUM CALM SEA CLEAR PALE SKY LOOKING SOUTH EAST

An abundance of
snow on the blue
mountains between
Hammerfest and
Øksfjord, virtually
white sky.

ROCKS JUST OUTSIDE ØKSFJORD FULL OF SMALL ALMOST VERTICAL SNOW FILLED RAVINES PLACID WATER + SKY 13/5/99 4.30PM

12/8

I loved the texture of the rocky shore just outside Øksfjord – small almost vertical snow filled gullies reflected partly in the placid water. I wondered if this dramatic scene would make a good book cover.

More lumpy rounded rocks of a grey/beige colour with afternoon shadows in purple/blue.

3.30 pm lumpy granite rocks. grey/beige purple/blue shadows.   Brian Gorazos   1272

LOOKING BACK ON ØKSFJORD 5.15 pm 13/3/99.
1500 METRES MOUNTAINS.

The scenery changed dramatically by the half hour; smooth snow covered tops and plunging ravines with tiny villages dotted along the coast. Made me realise how dependent the inhabitants are on water borne communication.

PULLING OUT OF ØKSFJORD 4.40pm 13/5/99 CONDITIONS AS ABOVE.

Another scene near
Øksfjord, I wrote
"Can't get enough of
the tranquillity and
silence – so serene".

48

And then jagged
toothed mountains
dived straight into the
sea. Overleaf is an
enlarged detail of the
right hand portion of
the sketch.

LOOKING FROM PRESBERGGRUNNEN WEATHER AS BEFORE 7.20 PM 13.5.99. NEARLY AT SKJERVØY.

SOUTH FROM HARSTAD 14/5/99 10AM.
NEXT STOP RISØYHAMN QUIET VILLAGE CALM WITH CONNECTING
HIGH BRIDGE LARGE SCHOOL + PLENTY OF SILVER BIRCH.
FLOWERS & TREES JUST COMING OUT. ACCESS VIA CHANNEL
DREDGED 1922.

We were surrounded by mountains and islands on all sides. Near here the waters are turquoise with pale yellow sand banks clearly visible from the ship.

Sometimes it seemed as though we were moving effortlessly through a heavenly dream. Ahead was Risøyhamn, a quiet village really but with a large school.

COMING OUT OF RISOYHAMN SAME CONDITIONS AS
PREVIOUS DAYS - HEADING FOR THE LOFOTEN ISLANDS.
NOON 14/5/99

12·25 PM 14/5/1999 PULLING FURTHER
AWAY FROM RISOYHAMN CONDITIONS
AS BEFORE BUT FINGERS GETTING TOO
COLD TO DRAW WILL MOVE INSIDE.

NEXT HARBOUR SORTLAND NICE CHURCH
BEHIND STATOIL TANKS SMALL
NAVY FRIGATE MORE FARMS &
GRASS LAND ALONG COAST.

12.25pm, 14/5/1999, I noted that the temperature was dropping, my fingers could hardly hold the pen, had to move inside. Headed towards Sortland through the dramatically narrow Raftsundet Straights. Sortland's nice church at odds with navy frigate and oil storage tanks. Soon we saw grass along the coast.

We took a bus at Svølvaer and travelled around the fertile Lofoten Islands, stopping all too shortly at a splendid gallery of fine local paintings in the village of Henningsvjaer, where houses are built over the water and racks full of dried cod are much in evidence. Could have spent an idyllic week here painting and drawing. Had to make do with my camera.

The captain sailed us into the small Trollfjord and kindly turned very slowly around – we were perilously close to the rocks. I couldn't make up my mind whether to draw, paint or photograph – I opted for the latter but still could not resist a quick doodle too.

TROLLFJORD BRIAN EDWARDS 1999.

"It spread a smile across the face of the water."

53

We rejoined the Polarlys at another fishing village – Stamsund. Here the old fishermen had wooden houses clustered around the jetties and warehouses; some are turned into holiday cottages – but there are still many cod racks.

HENNINGSVJAER, LOFOTEN   BRIAN EDWARDS. 14/5/99.

STAMSUND LOFOTEN ISLANDS   MAY 1999 BRIAN EDWARDS.
1999.

And then we pulled out into open sea, captivated by this huge chain of mountains silhouetted against a magnificent sunset. A few folk stopped up well into the night, savouring the view as it gradually receded.

6.35PM 9/5/99. APPROACHING STANSUND IN LOFOTEN ISLANDS

BRIAN EDWARDS

1252

The Lofotens slipped well astern and we woke up at Ørnes, closely surrounded, like a Swiss village, with high peaks. I wrote that the town itself is not distinguished apart from that magnificent setting. The weather appeared to be breaking up.

ØRNES 5/5/99 8AM.
PALE GREEN CLOUD COVER MEDIUM CALM SEA.
LOOKS LIKE THE WEATHER MAY BE
BREAKING UP. LOTS OF SMALL BLACK
FISH IN THE HARBOUR
TOWN NOT DISTINGUISHED APART
FROM SETTING.

1227

With another fishing station to one side, the clouds broke up to give us clear blue skies again just in time to welcome the globe perched on a small island and heralding the Arctic Circle. Much too busy sketching to have time for the onboard celebrations that the Norwegians enjoyed so energetically.

THE GLOBE SHOWS THE LINE OF THE ARCTIC CIRCLE 10AM 15/5/99. BLUE SKY STARTING TO SUPERCEDE THE GREY STRATUS.

My most lasting
memories are of
wonderful reflections
– of mountains,
boats and villages
duplicated upside
down in the calm
waters. How lucky
we remained with
the weather.

The Seven Sisters, the Helgeland Mountains, which rise to over 1000 metres (nearly 3500 feet), feature in the saga I describe on Page 64.

On this fine afternoon with clear blue sky the Sisters were wearing what must surely be a modesty veil of cloud.

THE SEVEN SISTERS PEAKS SHROUDED IN MIST.

Nesna was delightful but we had no time to explore as we were bound for the narrow harbour of Brønnøysund where a quarter mile bridge carries the road across to the Torghatten Mountain.

NESNA. 11.30 AM 15/5/99.

5.30 pm 15/5/99.
THE BRIDGE AT
BRØNNØYSUND

5.20 pm 15/5/99. BRØNNØYSUND
BRØNNØYSUND
1231

One of the most attractive advantages of travelling by the coastal steamer is the large number of villages and small towns served by Polarlys. Whenever we had a few minutes I would dive off and rush around capturing the environment with my camera. At other times I could only sketch from the ship. And then there were the unforgettable skies, day after day, night after night.

In all the villages, salted cod is hung up to dry – nailed to eaves or walls or in the larger, fishing communities, hung out on huge racks. Why don't the birds go for them? Is it the salt?

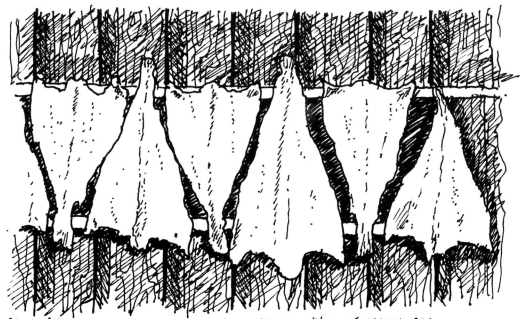

SALTED COD HUNG UP TO DRY OUT   LOFOTEN ISLANDS   BRIAN EDWARDS 1991.

112 M above sea level to hop.
1600m x 12 = 16 w x 25-30 h.

TORGHATTEN FROM THE NORTH HALF WAY UP NORWAY.   5.40 PM 15/5/95.   1272

Everyone on board looked forward to seeing the Torghatten, this extraordinary island mountain. I started to sketch from the panoramic lounge as we approached from the north at 5.40pm.

We had come around to the east, and on my second sketch of the Torghatten I was rewarded when two orca whales surfaced close by. I noted the time, it was 5.50pm, and sketched furiously away.

ORCA'S PLAYING OFF TORGHATTEN - 5.50 PM 15/5/95
FROM SOUTH EAST
1233

By 6 o'clock we had moved round to the south and I had taken up a standing position in the stern to pick out the 'arrow hole' in the hat. The opening runs right through the mountain (some 160 metres) and the floor is 112 metres from sea level. As the cave floor slopes up in a northerly direction there is a much better view of the opening from the south. This seven-minute sketch has been enlarged to show the detailed pen marks.

The Saga of the Helgeland Mountains is the much-varied tale of a man called Vågekallen who lived in the Lofoten Islands. He was thought of as a simpleton and as such, women ignored him. One day seven beautiful sisters, the daughters of a local king, were seen dancing naked in the fjord with the lovely Lekamøya. Vågkallen, on horseback, quite naturally chased after them but a knight called Hestamannen woke up and, in order to save Lekamøya for himself, shot an arrow at the Lofoten man. However all this was witnessed by another king who threw his hat to divert the arrow, which then pierced the headgear and fell into the sea. Too late, the major elements in the saga realised it was already sunset and they were turned to stone. Personally I think I am convinced that it is all a fairy story or am I?

The seven sisters are shown here on page 58, Hestamannen on page 24 and Torghatten (The Hat) on pages 62, 63 and this page.

MOUNTAINS ON TUSTNA
3·30pm 16/5/99.

1·35

The late afternoon light tended to throw the oddly shaped mountains into deep shadow making them even more menacing.

LIGHTHOUSE OUT OF CHRISTIANSUND 6pm 16/5/99.

Kristiansund has an equally odd shaped lighthouse.

off BUD 7pm 16/5/99. rougher seas exposing
The many groups of rocks with vigorous
white bases. cloud over mountains otherwise blue sky.

1704

Between Kristiansund and Molde we crossed sea unprotected by islands, whilst closer to shore, these jumping whales turned out to be nothing other than turned up waves in the now restless sea. The rocks here had a peculiarly humped shape like a prehistoric monster creeping into the sea. I began to see how the myths began.

NEAR SKALTUN 7.45 16/5/99
FRENA KOMM NEAR MOLDE

1205

Soon we were in
calmer waters as
we passed close to
Frena on our way
into Molde.

1286

THE HORSE
'10.15 17 MAY 1989
PLACID SEA LOTS OF
SMALL ISLANDS WITH
THE ROUND ROCKS &
LICHEN. NORWEGIAN
CONSTITUTION DAY PARADE
ROUND BOAT

The island of Alden called 'Norwegian Horse', 'Norwegian Lion' and 'The Blue Man,' by fishermen. The first two obviously refer to the strong shape and the latter to Alden's colour when it is silhouetted against the sunset.

NORWEGIAN LIGHTHOUSE BRIAN EDWARDS 1999

We should not forget, however, the important role that the hundreds of lighthouses, of all shapes and sizes, have played in making coastal navigation so much safer. Perhaps I have neglected them in this sketchbook – we often simply moved past too quickly.

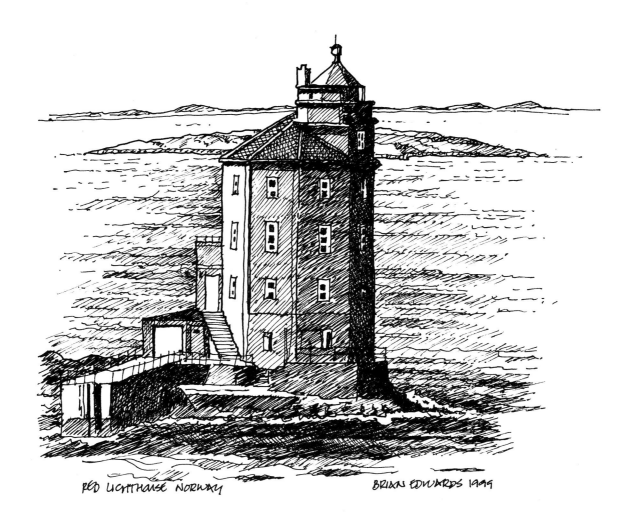

RED LIGHTHOUSE NORWAY   BRIAN EDWARDS 1999

Sometimes the lighthouses are tiny unmanned structures on the odd small rock, yet others are proud and multi-storey.

And so our journey was coming to an end as we moved up the channel leading to Bergen passing yet more bridges, including Norway's longest suspension example. Throughout our trip we had been impressed with the way that Norway has tackled the problems of communication in linking islands to each other and to the mainland, thus revolutionising travel in the coastal areas.

BRIDGE AT KLAUVANESET
1·45 pm MID CALM
THRO' CHANNEL TOWARDS
BERGEN.

Sadly this 'Old Bergen' Museum of preserved houses and shops was closed, it was Constitution Day. Our disappointment was compensated for by the vast numbers of folk in traditional costume parading around the streets. We did manage to wander around the outside of these lovely old wooden houses however.

BERGEN OLD MUSEUM
BRIKNEDNAKDIS 1999.

1396.

I was particularly taken by this old fire station as we walked around the hilly Sandviken area of Bergen with its steep cobbled streets and old, bravely coloured wooden houses.

OLD FIRE STATION? BERGEN BE. 1999.

CONSTITUTION DAY BERGEN MAY 1999 BRAVELLARDS

SOME NOTES ON MY SKETCHING

ADVENTUROUS CHURCH NORWAY BRIAN EDWARDS

SILVER BIRCHES NEAR TROMSO BRIAN EDWARDS 1999

Although I sketched and painted much of the time we were on board, despite the light and long evenings, I had to sleep! So I missed some views. Sketching on a moving vessel is not easy. During most days I spent hours working from the sheltered rear deck and that created quite a problem. For as we moved along we sailed in and out of islands, some of which quickly obscured the very scene I was recording. Thus speed was of the essence, although I have over the years drawn much faster as time becomes more unrepeatable and our health more susceptible. Most of my work illustrated here is not intended as "finished" except for a few which were later completed from photographs. In the evenings, after dinner, Pam and I usually sat up front in the panoramic lounge where I could sketch in comparative warmth. At least I had a clear view of what lay ahead.

Mainly I worked with Rotring Rapidograph technical pens of varying line thickness, using Rotring waterproof black ink. I also, on a few occasions, used a black ballpoint. Colour was added in some cases and for that I had Caran d'Ache Prismalo coloured pencils, and for better or worse, I licked my thumb and then smeared the colour quickly across the drawing. Occasionally I used a small watercolour 'Pochette' set from Winsor and Newton, generally with a thickish brush no.10 Cotman series. I had a selection of small drawing pads (ring bound ones are preferable), with medium weight, fairly smooth paper. I am very fortunate that although I live in a historic peakland village, I am not far away from Pinders of Sheffield, my trusted and helpful suppliers for some forty years or more; sometimes I think they put as much energy into my drawings as I do.

My recent work has become more immediate and, although I dislike the word, impressionistic. The subject is analysed in parallel with the painting, which is often of mixed media. My next project will hopefully result in a book of illustrations covering the area north of Lake Geneva and timed to coincide with the launch of an exhibition near Lausanne in the spring of 2001.

Incidentally I never use a pencil to sketch out a composition first. I prefer to go straight in with pen or brush – that gives much more freedom and increases confidence. I also find that the sensitive barrel point of the drawing pens can pick up pencil dust and that leads to clogging. On the rare occasions I work in pencil, I shun the security of an eraser.

In my classes I always emphasise the need to look and understand the subject and, of course, this becomes a faster exercise as time goes by.

NEAR BUD 6.40 16/5/99.

1203

This page was sketched as a few-minute demonstration, for a small group of English ladies, with some discussion about working methods and tonal perspective. On the previous page I have had my original sketch of the 'Seven Sisters' on Page 57 enlarged over 300%, so you can see that my sketching could be described as simply scribbling!

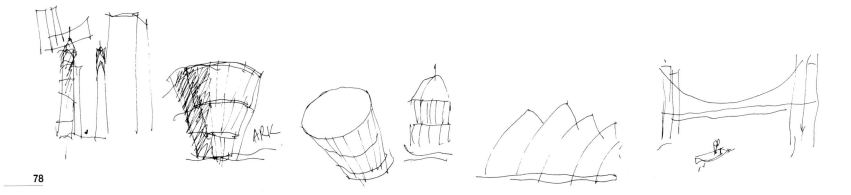

BRIAN EDWARDS. TURNING ROUND IN TROLLFJORD MAY 1999

My sketching was made fairly easy by the smoothness of the journey that was undoubtedly due to the fine May weather and placid seas we experienced. However I was amazed at the precision steering of the ship and this was wonderfully demonstrated when the Polarlys turned around "on a sixpence" in the Trollfjord, missing the rock face by a hairsbreadth and giving us the opportunity to experience this cavernous fjord at **very** close hand.

Well, we returned to England with very fond views of Norway, its friendly people and fine food. We will, without doubt, return. I hope you have enjoyed this sketchbook and perhaps next time you're choosing a holiday you might follow in our wake – I have no doubt that it will be worth it. In the meantime I'll leave the frozen, very far, North Cape to the Samis (Lapps) and reindeer.

LAPP FOR THE TOURISTS NEAR NORTH CAPE MAY 1999
BRIAN EDWARDS.
12.90

ACKNOWLEDGEMENTS

I would like to acknowledge the help of the following:

My wife Pam for her usual encouragement and enthusiasm, and for help with the word processing. I now openly confess that this stunning cruise was her idea. Arvid and Ingebjørg Tjeldnes for persuading me to produce the book and for giving me a running commentary on our voyage and for teaching me the secret of longevity – 'every day is an opportunity'. Laura Tuttle, our multilingual and diplomatic tour manager, and the many fellow passengers, Norwegian, English, American and Canadian, who expressed their interest in my sketches. The crew of the Polarlys for making the journey so enjoyable and for serving such frostbite-proof and delicious food. Our tour organisers, Titon HiTours of Redhill, Barry Ford of Scandinavian Travel Service for additional help and Bakewell Travel for introducing us to the cruise. Keith Stubley and the staff at Northends who printed the book and were most helpful in dealing with artwork so skilfully. Maureen Gee for additional word processing. My old mate Mike Ford for the very flattering photograph used on the back cover of this book, and Pinders of Sheffield.

A LONG HOUSE ON THE LOFOTEN ISLANDS   RF. 99.

INDEX

USE FOR A STATUE
TROMSØ MAY 1999
BRIANEDWARDS

1291